A New True Book

EUROPE

By D. V. Georges

CHILDRENS PRESS ®

CHICAGO

The Louvre, Paris, France

PHOTO CREDITS

© Cameramann International, Ltd.—21, 24 (right), 31 (left), 40 (left), 42 (right), 43

© Joseph A. DiChello Jr.—12 (bottom left), 28 (right)

© Joan Dunlop—13 (left)

© Gartman Agency—35 (left)

Image Finders: © Bob Skelly—9 (bottom left), 33 (left)

Nawrocki Stock Photo: © Michael Fox—45 (top right)

Odyssey Productions: © Robert Frerck—31 (right)

© Chip & Rosa Maria Peterson—2, 13 (right), 45 (left)

Photri: © J. Allen Cash—12 (right), 14 (right)

H. Armstrong Roberts, Inc.—17 (left), 39 (left), 45 (bottom right)
© Camerique—33 (right)
© Geisser—29 (bottom right)
© J. Messerschmidt—9 (right)
© M. Spector—45 (top left)
© M. Thonig—Cover, 22 (right), 29 (bottom left)
© ZEFA—10 (left)

Root Resources: © Ruth Weltz—19

© M. B. Rosalsky—38 (2 photos)

© Bob & Ira Spring—17 (right), 29 (top), 34 (left), 37

Valan Photos:
© Pierre R. Chabot—27 (left)
© Kennon Cooke—12 (top left)
© Herman H. Giethoorn—14 (left)
© H. C. Howes—40 (right)
© T. Joyce—22 (left), 25 (2 photos)
© Klaus Werner—9 (top left)

Worldwide Photo: © Alexander Chabe—10 (right), 24 (left), 34 (right), 36 (right), 41 (left)

© Jerome Wyckoff—35 (right)

Maps—Albert R. Magnus, 6, 11, 13, 15, 17, 20, 27, 28, 30, 36, 39, 41, 42

Cover: Neuschwanstein Castle in Allgau, West Germany

Library of Congress Cataloging-in-Publication Data

Georges, D. V.
  Europe.

  (A New true book)
  Includes index.
  Summary: Locates Europe, divides it into six areas including the British Isles, Scandinavia, West Europe, the Alps, Peninsulas of the Mediterranean, and East Europe, and describes the people, cities, and geographical features of each.
  1. Europe—Description and travel—1971-   — Juvenile literature. [1. Europe—Description and travel] I. Title.
D923.G47 1986   914   86-9585
ISBN 0-516-01292-4

TABLE OF CONTENTS

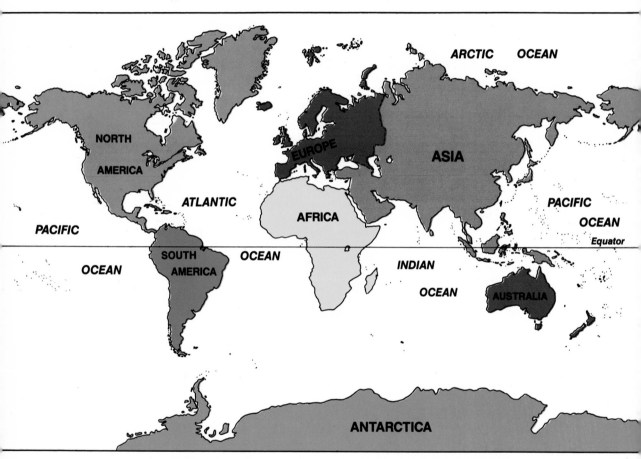

Australia is an island continent.

FINDING EUROPE

The seven continents are the largest masses of land on earth. Two of the continents—Australia and Antarctica—are surrounded by water. Three others— North America, South America, and Africa—are almost surrounded by water.

But Asia and Europe are different. They are connected by four thousand miles of land and seas.

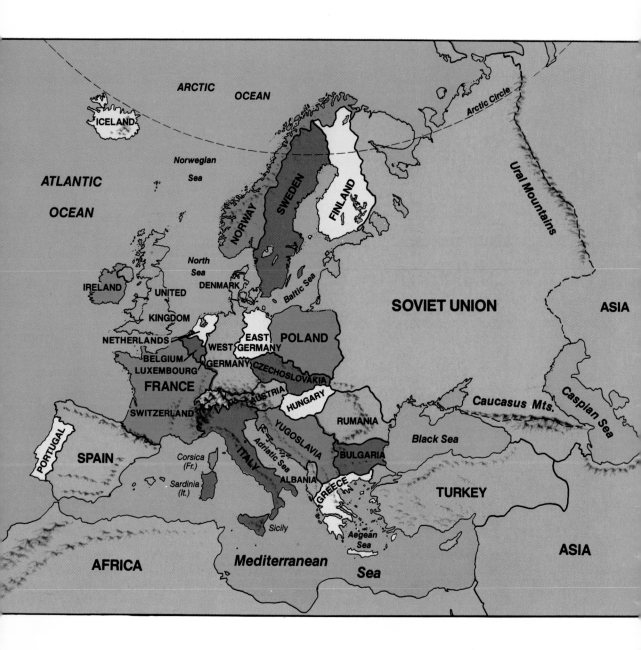

Europe is west of Asia. It is the sixth-largest continent. Europe is the size of Canada.

The border between Europe and Asia stretches from the Ural Mountains through the Caspian Sea. From there, the border goes through the Caucasus Mountains, the Black Sea, Turkey, and the Aegean Sea.

THE BRITISH ISLES

Great Britain and Ireland are the largest of the British Isles. England, Scotland, and Wales are on the same island.

Between Great Britain and the north of France lies the English Channel. Every day, ferryboats carry people, cars, and trains across the channel.

Hovercraft leaves Dover, England for Calais, France across the English Channel (top left). Tower Bridge (left) is in London, the capital of the United Kingdom, which includes England, Wales, Scotland, and Northern Ireland. Dublin (above) is the capital of Ireland.

London is in southeast Great Britain. The Thames River winds through the city. Within London, more than twenty-five bridges cross the Thames!

London is the home of

Parliament (above) with the clock, Big Ben, at right. Welsh Royal Guards (right) parade in front of Buckingham Palace daily.

Big Ben, Westminster Abbey, and Buckingham Palace.

East of London, the Thames River meets the North Sea. Thus, London is an important port. From London, ships can travel

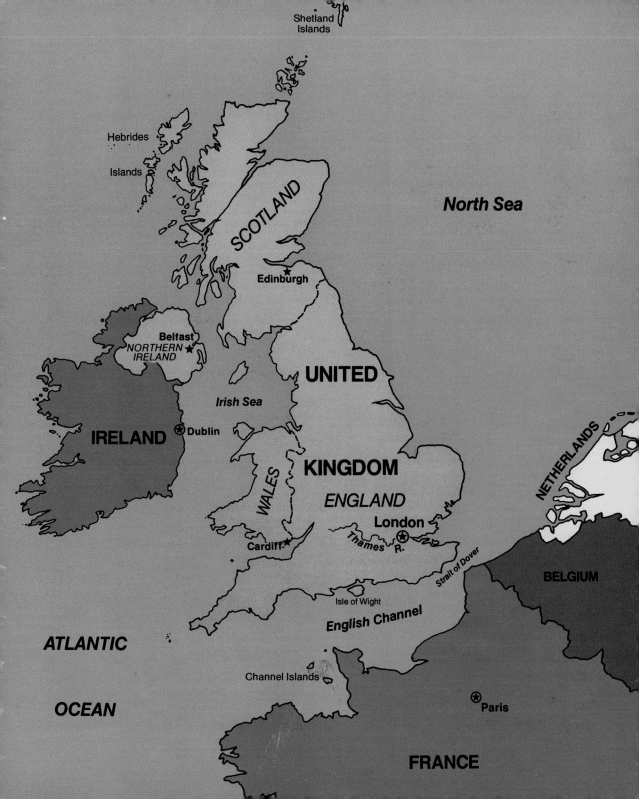

north through the North
Sea or south through the
English Channel to the
Atlantic Ocean.
Rolling plains and low
mountains cover most of

Countryside in southern Wales (left),
rural homes in County Mayo, Ireland (below
left), Donan Castle on the banks of Loch Duich
in the highlands of Scotland (below)

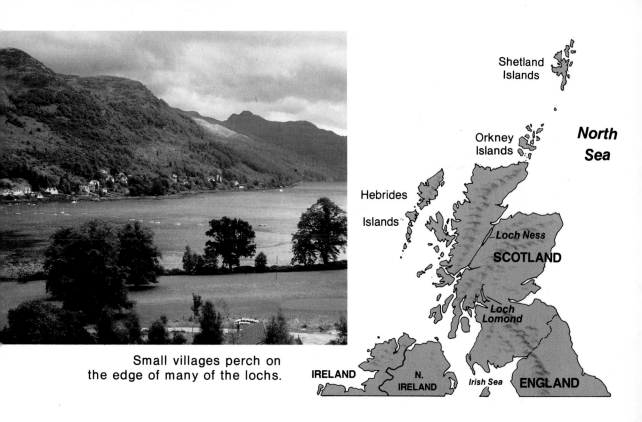

Small villages perch on the edge of many of the lochs.

the British Isles. The mountains are called highlands. In Scotland, the highlands are scenic and rugged. Lochs are long, deep lakes in the highlands of Scotland.

Shetland pony (left), woman (right) spinning

The Hebrides are a group of five hundred islands northwest of Scotland. The Shetlands are one hundred islands north of Scotland.

People who live on the islands fish and raise sheep for wool. Knits and tweeds made on the islands are sold all over the world.

SCANDINAVIA

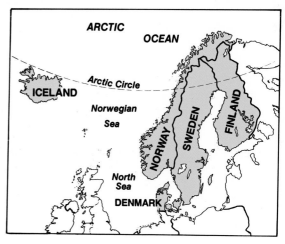

Iceland, Norway, Sweden, Finland, and Denmark are countries of Scandinavia in northern Europe.

One thousand years ago, Scandinavia was the home of Vikings. Vikings were great warriors and seafarers. They traveled far—a few times, even to North America.

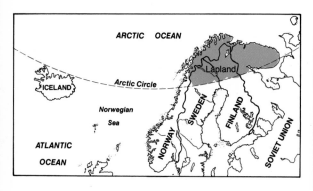

Copenhagen, Denmark

The first Vikings lived in Denmark and the south of Norway and Sweden. Later they settled in Iceland, an island six hundred miles west of Norway.

About ten percent of Iceland is covered with ice. There are many volcanoes and hot springs. The hot springs are used for power and heat.

Greenhouses are heated by natural hot springs in Iceland (above). The Lapp family (left) wears traditional dress.

The Arctic Circle touches northern Iceland. It also passes through the north part of Norway, Sweden, and Finland. The land region north of the Arctic Circle is called Lapland.

Lapps are the people of Lapland. They raise

reindeer for food and
hides. Lapps also use
reindeer for travel. On the
coasts, Lapps fish in the
icy waters.

Rugged mountains
stretch from Lapland to the
south of Norway. High in
the mountains, layers of
ice and snow form
glaciers.

Deep valleys along the
west coast of Norway were
once full of glaciers. The
glaciers melted and
seawater filled the valleys.

Fjord in Norway

The sea inlets are called fjords.

There are thousands of fjords. Tourists come from distant parts to see the fjords of Norway.

WESTERN EUROPE

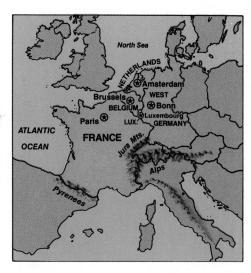

France, Belgium, The Netherlands, and West Germany are in western Europe. Luxembourg is a tiny country between France and West Germany.

Fertile plains cover much of western Europe. There are also several mountain chains.

The Pyrenees separate Spain from France.

The Jura Mountains lie
between France and West
Germany. In southwest
France, the Pyrenees form
the border with Spain. The
Alps touch southeast
France and the south of
West Germany.

On the hilly slopes of France and West Germany, many kinds of grapes grow. The grapes are made into wine. France and West Germany are famous for wines they produce.

Cheese market in Alkmarr, The Netherlands (below). Stahleck Castle in the Rhine Valley, West Germany (right).

Dairy cattle are raised throughout western Europe. Fine cheeses come from the dairy farms of France and The Netherlands.

Cities of western Europe are hundreds of years old. They are full of great museums, lovely parks, and beautiful buildings. The cities attract tourists from all over the world.

In The Netherlands, the port of Amsterdam has many canals and bridges.

Canal in the city of Amsterdam (above).
Ships, large and small, may move down this
canal (right) into the North Sea.

Canals join Amsterdam
with the North Sea. Canals
also join Amsterdam with
the Rhine River, the longest
river in western Europe.

Paris is the capital of
France. The most famous
buildings of Paris are

The Eiffel Tower (left) and the Notre Dame Cathedral are two of the most famous landmarks in Paris, France.

Notre Dame Cathedral, the Louvre Museum, and the Eiffel Tower. The Eiffel Tower is almost one thousand feet high. Visitors can see all of Paris from the observation deck at the top.

THE ALPS

The Alps are mountains in central Europe. Switzerland and Austria are the main countries of the Alps. However, the Alps extend into northern Italy and part of France and West Germany.

Liechtenstein is a very small country between Switzerland and Austria.

People travel to the Alps for the scenic landscapes and winter sports.

The Matterhorn, Switzerland

The highest peak in the Alps is Mont Blanc. It rises 15,771 feet.

Other great peaks of the Alps are the Matterhorn and Grossglockner.

When glaciers high in the Alps melt, large lakes

27

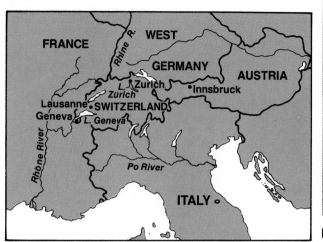

Farm in the Austrian mountains

and rivers form. The Rhone
River flows west to France
and the Rhine River flows
north to Germany.

Many cities in Switzerland
are on the shores of lakes.
Lausanne and Geneva are on
Lake Geneva. Zurich, on
Lake Zurich, is the largest
city in Switzerland.

Aletsch Glacier (top) is the longest glacier in Switzerland. The cities of Geneva (left) and Zurich (above)

PENINSULAS OF THE MEDITERRANEAN

The Mediterranean Sea borders three important peninsulas of Europe. They are the Iberian Peninsula, the Italian Peninsula, and the Balkan Peninsula.

30

A mountain village in Andalusia, Spain (left) and a beach along the coast

There are many mountains on the peninsulas. Summers there are warm and dry, while winters are cool and rainy.

Portugal, Spain, and tiny Andorra are on the Iberian Peninsula. The Atlantic Ocean lies to the west of the Iberian Peninsula.

Punta Marroqui is the southernmost point in Europe. It is on the Strait of Gibraltar. North Africa lies just across the strait.

The Rock of Gibraltar juts out into the Mediterranean Sea. Monkeys called Barbary apes live on the Rock of Gibraltar. This is the only place in Europe where monkeys live!

Nearly eight hundred miles across the

Barbary apes (left) live on
the Rock of Gibraltar (above).

Mediterranean from Spain
lies the boot-shaped Italian
Peninsula.

Italy is on the Italian
Peninsula. The islands of
Sicily and Sardinia are also
part of Italy. North of

33

Hikers on Mount Vesuvius (above). The Ponte Vecchio, or "Old Bridge," crosses the Arno River in Florence, Italy (right).

Sardinia, the island of Corsica belongs to France.

The Apennine Mountains cover the length of the Italian Peninsula.

In southern Italy there are active volcanoes. Mount Vesuvius is near Naples. It has had many

Canals in Venice (left). The ruins
of the Roman Forum (above) in Rome

eruptions. In A.D. 79 lava
from an eruption buried
the city of Pompeii.

Rome, Florence, and
Venice are historic cities in
Italy. Palaces and churches
in these cities hold great
works of art.

In Rome, there are also
ruins from the days of the

The Colosseum in Rome

Roman Empire. The Roman Forum and the Colosseum are the most famous ruins.

The Adriatic Sea separates the Italian Peninsula from the west coast of the Balkan Peninsula. Yugoslavia, Rumania, Bulgaria, Albania, and Greece are countries of the Balkan Peninsula.

The Acropolis in Athens

Greece is the most southern country. Tourists visit Greece because of the many beautiful islands. Also, there are ruins from the ancient Greek civilization.

Athens is the capital of Greece. In Athens, the Acropolis rises several

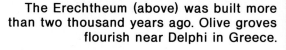
The Erechtheum (above) was built more than two thousand years ago. Olive groves flourish near Delphi in Greece.

hundred feet above the city. Ruins of ancient temples are on the Acropolis. The Parthenon and the Erechtheum are the largest temples.

Athens is an important port. Olives, cheese, and wine from Greece are shipped to many other countries.

Prague is the capital
of Czechoslovakia.

EASTERN EUROPE

East Germany, Poland,
Czechoslovakia, and
Hungary are countries of
eastern Europe.

One fourth of the Soviet
Union is also in eastern
Europe. This part of the

Coal mine (left) in Katowice, Poland. The General Headquarters in Leningrad (right)

Soviet Union has many factories and mines. Most Soviet people live here.

The Soviet Union has fifteen republics. Russia is the largest. The entire Soviet Union often is called Russia.

Leningrad and Moscow are the largest cities of

St. Basil's Cathedral in Moscow

the Soviet Union. Leningrad is a port in the northwest, near Scandinavia.

Moscow is the capital of the Soviet Union. Saint Basil's Cathedral in Moscow is known for its towers.

There are fertile plains in the western Soviet Union.

Traditional country home in Poland

The plains stretch into Poland and East Germany. Farmers grow wheat, sugar beets, and potatoes.

South of the plains, the Carpathian Mountains rise through much of Czechoslovakia. Coal and iron are mined in the Carpathian Mountains.

The Danube River cuts through Budapest, Hungary.

The famous Danube River forms part of the border between Czechoslovakia and Hungary.

Budapest—the capital of Hungary—is on the Danube River.

NEW AND OLD
MEET IN EUROPE

Cities of Europe are rich in history. Some cities have old ruins. Others have great art from the past.

Europe is important in today's world. Much culture—art, music, and ballet—still comes from Europe. Also, many cities of Europe are world centers for banks and industries.

In Europe, new and old blend side by side.

Piccadilly Circus (top left) in London, sidewalk cafe in Paris (top right), Reykjavik, Iceland (below left), Stockholm, Sweden (below right)

WORDS YOU SHOULD KNOW

A.D. — years after the death of Christ

Arctic Circle (ARK • tik SIR • kil) — an imaginary geographical circle in the far north of the earth

cathedral (kath • EE • dril) — a large, important church

ferryboat (FAIR • ee • bote) — a special boat for taking people, cars, trucks, and trains across a body of water

fertile (FER • til) — land that is dark, rich, and good for farming

fjord (FEE • yord) — a sea inlet that fills a deep glacier valley

glaciers (GLAY • sherz) — slowly moving layers of ice and snow that start out high in the mountains

hot springs (HAHT SPRINGZ) — hot water from underground that flows up to the earth's surface

lava (LAH • vah) — melted rock that erupts from a volcano

loch (LAHK) — a deep, narrow lake of Scotland

peninsula (pen • IN • soo • lah) — land that has water on three sides and is connected to a larger mass of land

ruins (ROO • inz) — what is left of buildings from long ago

seafarers (SEE • fair • erz) — people who sail on ships to distant lands

slopes (SLOHPEZ) — the sides of mountains

tweed (TWEED) — a thick wool cloth used to make suits and coats

Vikings (VYE • kingz) — people of Scandinavia who sailed the oceans and conquered new lands

volcano (vol • KAY • no) — a mountain that sometimes erupts with melted rock and steam

warrior (WAR • ee • or) — a person who fights wars and tries to conquer others

MAJOR COUNTRIES IN EUROPE

Name	Capitol	Name	Capital
Albania	Tiranë	Liechtenstein	Vaduz
Andorra	Andorra	Luxembourg	Luxembourg
Austria	Vienna	Malta	Valletta
Belgium	Brussels	Monaco	Monaco
Bulgaria	Sofia	Netherlands	Amsterdam
Czechoslovakia	Prague	Norway	Oslo
Denmark	Copenhagen	Poland	Warsaw
Finland	Helsinki	Portugal	Lisbon
France	Paris	Rumania	Bucharest
Germany (East)	Berlin (East)	Russia (European)	Moscow
Germany (West)	Bonn	San Marino	San Marino
Great Britain	London	Spain	Madrid
Greece	Athens	Sweden	Stockholm
Hungary	Budapest	Switzerland	Bern
Iceland	Reykjavik	Turkey (European)	Ankara
Ireland	Dublin	Vatican City	
Italy	Rome	Yugoslavia	Belgrade

INDEX

About the author

D.V. Georges is a geophysicist in Houston, Texas. Dr. Georges attended Rice University, earning a masters degree in chemistry in 1975 and a doctorate in geophysics in 1978.